BEEKEEPING FOR BEGINNERS

by
Andrew Richards

photography by
John Phipps

published by
Northern Bee Books
Scout Bottom Farm, Mytholmroyd, Hebden Bridge
West Yorkshire

Published in October 1991 by
Northern Bee Books,
Scout Bottom Farm,
Mytholmroyd,
Hebden Bridge,
West Yorkshire HX7 5JS.

Photographs by John Phipps.

Text © Andrew Richards.
Photos © John Phipps.

I S B N   0-907908-61-6

A CIP catalogue record for this book
is available from the British Library.

Printed by The Arc & Throstle Press,
Nanholme Mill,
Shaw Wood Road,
Todmorden,
Lancashire OL14 6DA.

Book Design by Karen Sutcliffe.

CONTENTS

PHOTOGRAPHS

Chapter 1

HOW MUCH, HOW MUCH AND HOW MUCH ?

This short first chapter tells you about the amount of **TIME** you will need to spend on beekeeping, what it will **COST** and what **RETURN** you can expect.

The operations and items discussed in this chapter are all described in detail later. This chapter is only here to give you a general idea of time, cost and what you can expect to get out of beekeeping.

▼ HOW MUCH TIME WILL IT TAKE ?

You can spend much more time than the minimum required, in particular while you are learning. The times given here are approximate minimum times for an experienced beekeeper and are given only as a general indication .

The minimum time you need to spend varies a great deal throughout the year. Bees, unlike other livestock, require very little attention in winter. They never require daily attention and you can usually vary the times that you need to attend to them to suit your own commitments.

The following guidelines give times for the main operations:

May	Spring cleaning	1 hour per hive

This will make life much easier through the rest of the year

May to August	Checking for swarm preparations, preventing swarming and adding per hive at 5 to honey storage space.	10 to 20 minutes 9 day intervals
June/July	Removing and extracting oil seed rape honey (if any)	2 hours per hive
September	Removing and extracting main honey crop.	2/3 hours per hive
September	Feeding sugar syrup for winter stores	10 minutes per hive 3 times at one week intervals
October	Fitting mouse guards	10 minutes per hive
October to May	Checking adequate stores available in hive	5 minutes per hive at 2/4 week intervals
May	Stimulative spring feeding	10 minutes per hive 2 or 3 times at 1 week intervals

There are some items which you will need to spend time on but not at any particular time of year.

You will need to allocate time to the construction of equipment, particularly hive parts and frames for the combs, which are usually supplied in "*kit*" form. These items are also available "*ready made up*" but at higher cost.

The preparation, packaging (including bottling) and marketing of your produce will also take time.

If you are going to move your bees between different forage sources, you will need time both to prepare them for the move and for the actual move itself.

▼ HOW MUCH WILL IT COST ?

The best sources of information on both cost and equipment available are the equipment manufacturers and suppliers catalogues.

The costs given here are for new equipment and based on 1991 prices.

Good secondhand equipment, when available, is usually about half of the new price.

The cost of a nucleus stock from a local beekeeper will be much less than the cost from an equipment supplier, probably a little more than half of the price.

If you can "*take*" a stray swarm yourself the bees will be free but you will need to get them checked to be sure that they are free of any disease.

The equipment suppliers usually offer a basic set of the essential protective clothing, tools, and one hive. This is often listed in their catalogues as a "*Beginners' Outfit*".

A beginners' outfit costs about £190

You should note that the beginners' outfit hardly ever contains sufficient honey storage chambers (or supers) and you will almost certainly want at least two hives.

A more realistic costing for starting with one hive is given on the next page.

▼ STARTING COSTS

Protective Clothing:

Hat and Veil	£ 12
Soft leather gloves with gauntlets	£ 18

Tools:

Smoker	£ 20
Hive tool	£ 6

Equipment:

A complete hive with two honey storage chambers including frames and wax foundation	£144

Bees:

A nucleus stock of bees from a local beekeeper	£ 35
Total	£235

The use of a honey extractor can be avoided by limiting honey production to cut comb or sections, see Chapter 2. You will probably decide to get one eventually and the cost will depend on:

- the size (number of frames extracted in one operation)
- construction material (polythene or stainless steel)
- power source (manual or electric)

For small scale operations the cost range is £100 to £350

▼ HOW MUCH WILL THE RETURN BE ?

The honey crop varies from year to year depending on the weather conditions. There is also a considerable variation from hive to hive. The following figures are a very rough guide for the surplus which can be removed leaving 30 to 50lbs for the bees winter requirements.

Averages of 40lbs are reasonable for a hive kept at one location.
In a poor year the average can be as low as 10lbs.
In a good year the average can be as high as 70lbs.

For comparison with the starting cost, the retail price of blossom honey in 1991 is about £2 per pound.

Chapter 2

The Basics

This chapter gives you some basic information on bees, hives, and the materials that bees collect/produce.

If you already know these basics you can skip this section and go straight to Chapter 3 Your *'Options and Objectives.'*

▼ THE BEES

A honeybee colony comprises:

- one fertile female (**THE QUEEN**),
- tens of thousands of infertile females (**WORKERS**)
- and several hundred males (**DRONES**).

The queen mates in flight. Mating flights take place on several occasions within the space of a few days during the first few weeks of her life.

She stores the drone sperm in her body and fertilises the eggs destined to become workers as they are laid.

The queen does not fertilise the eggs destined to become drones.
STOP, go back and read that again, its true, drones are related only to the queen and not to the drones that she mated with.

The Stages of Development

The queen lays **EGGS** in wax cells in the hive. Smaller cells (5 per inch) for eggs destined to become workers, larger cells (4 per inch) for eggs destined to become drones.

The eggs take three days to hatch into small grubs known as **LARVAE**

Young worker bees feed the worker larvae for five days and the drone larvae for six days. The food is a special *"brood food"* for two days and then a dilute honey and pollen mixture. During this time the larvae grow until they fill the cell, an increase in weight of 1500 times. When this stage is reached the worker bees seal the cell with wax and the larvae **PUPATE** which means that they change from a grub into an insect.

The changes in the sealed cell,which include pupation, take seven days for a queen, thirteen days for a worker and fifteen days for a drone. After this time the adult bee bites its way out of the cell and joins the colony.

Worker bees spend the first part of their life performing hive duties. Starting with cleaning out the cells vacated by other emerging bees and progressing through feeding the larvae and comb construction to guard duty. At about four weeks they start to make short flights from the hive and become foragers.

▼ HIVES

There are many different types of hive. some of these types and their advantages/ disadvantages for particular applications will be described later. All modern hives are variations on a basic design which is described here.

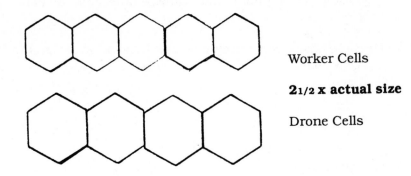

Worker Cells

21/2 **x actual size**

Drone Cells

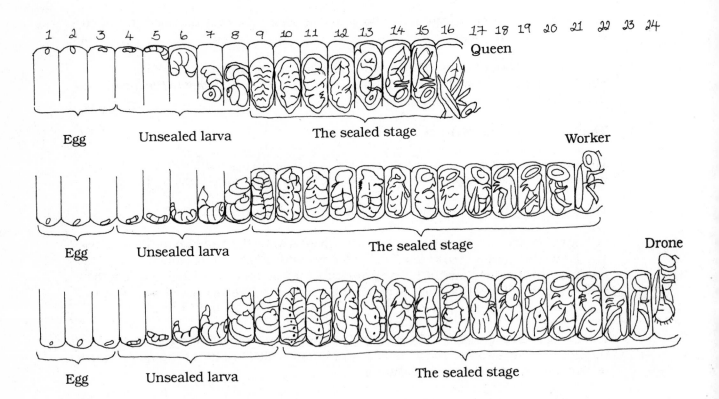

The different rates of development from eggs to be for queen, worker and drone. The number of days, apart from the egg stage, are average; they can be lengthened according to hive and weather conditions.

The hive comprises two main sections:

1 The **BROOD CHAMBER** where the queen lays eggs and the larvae (brood) are raised.

2 The honey storage chambers normally called **SUPERS.**

These two sections are separated with a mesh which is large enough to allow the passage of worker bees but not large enough to allow the queen through. This mesh is known as the **QUEEN EXCLUDER.**

The **BROOD CHAMBER** which contains the brood nest is mounted on a **FLOOR BOARD**. The floor board has raised sides and back with an opening at the front to provide the only entrance and exit for the bees.

The honey storage supers are covered with a **COVER BOARD** (sometimes called a crown board) and the whole thing is covered with a weatherproof **ROOF**.

The Queen Excluder

Roof

Cover Board

Honey Storage Chamber (Super)

Queen Excluder

Brood Chamber

Floor

▼ INSIDE THE HIVE

The brood chamber (or brood box) and honey storage supers contain wooden **FRAMES** which hang from a ledge cut into the top of each box. Each wooden frame is fitted with a sheet of beeswax **FOUNDATION** which is impressed with the natural shape of the cells.

The bees construct combs of wax cells on this foundation using the wax they produce from glands on the underside of their bodies. The resulting framed combs allow the beekeeper to remove individual combs for inspection.

A typical frame from the brood chamber showing sealed brood below an arch of sealed honey.

A typical frame from the honey storage super

The embedded wire helps to keep the comb fixed in the frame when it is being examined.

The wax foundation is normally strengthened by having wire embedded in it. This helps to keep the comb fixed into the frame both when it is removed from the hive to be examined and when the honey is being extracted in a centrifugal honey extractor.

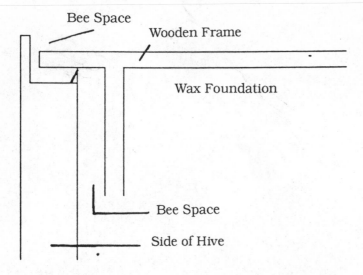

Bee Space

Wooden Frame

Wax Foundation

Bee Space

Side of Hive

▼ THE BEE SPACE

Spaces are left in the hive to provide access for the bees to all parts.

The spaces are between the frames and the sides of hive, and between the tops of the frames in one chamber and the bottom of the frames in the chamber above.

If the spaces are more than 3/8 inch, the bees will build wax comb in them. This comb is known as **BRACE COMB.**

A cover board which has been too close to the frames showing the outline of the frame tops where they have been joined with propolis.

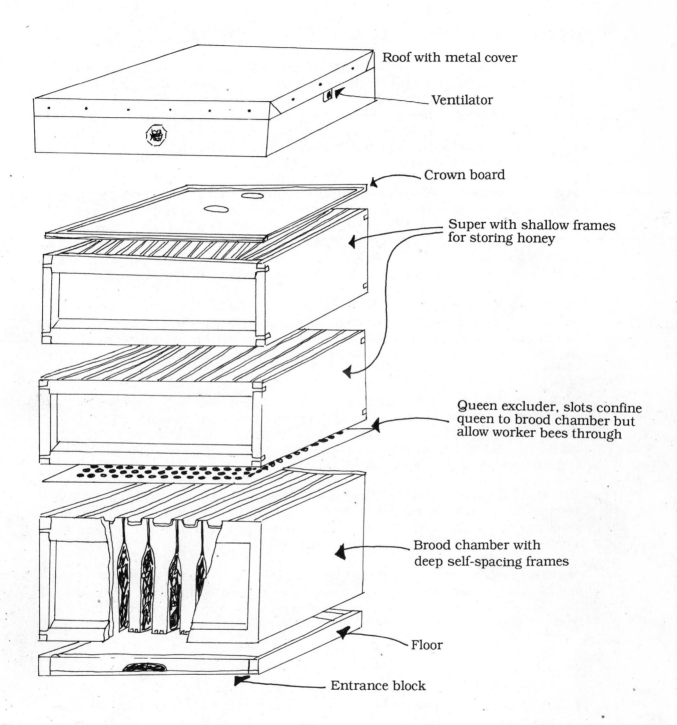

Roof with metal cover

Ventilator

Crown board

Super with shallow frames for storing honey

Queen excluder, slots confine queen to brood chamber but allow worker bees through

Brood chamber with deep self-spacing frames

Floor

Entrance block

The hive complete with frames

If the spaces are less than 3/16 inch, the bees will fill them with a substance called propolis (propolis is explained below).

Brace comb and propolis cause unnecessary difficulty when examining a hive. Accurate construction of the hive is therefore necessary to maintain 1/4 inch spacing

▼ THE MATERIALS THAT BEES COLLECT/PRODUCE

The main material collected is **NECTAR**. Nectar is a weak solution of sugars (mainly fructose and glucose) found in the flowers of plants. The bees convert the nectar into **HONEY** by using an enzyme and by evaporating the surplus water. The honey is food for the adult bees, some being is stored in wax cells for use in winter. The amount stored is usually more than the 30 to 50lbs required for winter food by the colony and the surplus is available for the beekeeper. You will find some information about honey and honey production on the next page.

POLLEN is also collected by bees from flowers and stored in wax cells. Pollen has a very high protein content and is mixed with dilute honey by the bees to feed their larvae. For this reason it is an important material for the development of the colony particularly in the spring. While the beekeeper is not usually able to plant sufficient nectar yielding crops to produce honey, it is possible to assist colony development by providing pollen sources. Pollen can be used as a food and is collected by some beekeepers.

PROPOLIS is the sticky substance which covers the buds of some trees. This substance is collected by bees to cement the movable parts of the hive together and to block up any gaps. Propolis has antibiotic properties, its natural function is to protect the tree buds it covers. For this reason it has medicinal uses and it is collected for sale by some beekeepers.

WAX is produced by bees from glands on the underside of their body. The bees use this wax to construct their combs of cells. Beeswax has many uses e.g. high quality furniture cream and polish, candles and wax comb foundation for beekeepers. Beekeeping equipment suppliers will buy wax. Surplus wax is collected by most beekeepers either for their own use or for sale.

ROYAL JELLY is the special food produced by bees to feed queen larvae. It normally occurs in very small quantities, however the bees can be induced to raise queens and thus increase production. Royal jelly production is a specialised operation, it is produced commercially in China and the far east.

WATER is another material collected by bees. Although it is not one of the usable products, it is needed by the colony to dilute honey for feeding the larvae. Water is also used to cool the hive in hot weather. The provision of a water supply is another way in which the beekeeper can usefully help the bee colony.

▼ HONEY

As honey is the main product of beekeeping you should know something about its characteristics and the different forms it can be produced and marketed in.

Honey is produced by bees from the nectar of flowering plants and trees. Each type of plant produces a different nectar in the same way that each type of fruit tree produces different fruit. When the honey is first produced it is in the viscous liquid state. The combs of honey are usually removed from the hive while the honey is still in this liquid state.

Almost all honey will crystallise (usually called granulation) at some later time. The time taken to granulate depends on two factors, the nectar source and the storage temperature. Honey from the brascia family, in particular from oil seed rape, granulates particularly quickly (days). The honey from most other sources takes many months to granulate. Granulated honey can be returned to the liquid state by gentle heating. The temperature of the honey should not be allowed to exceed 120 °F as this will destroy some of its constituents. As honey is a poor conductor of heat it is advisable to heat the container in a waterbath at lower temperatures, say 100 °F. It is also important to loosen the lid of the container to prevent a sticky explosion as it expands.

Honey, extracted from the combs in a centrifugal extractor, can be stored in jars either in the liquid state or in the **CREAMED** state. Creamed honey is honey which has granulated, been softened with heat and then stirred so that there is not enough liquid between the crystals to allow more crystals to form. Creamed honey should remain in a soft state for a long period of time (years).

Cut comb honey is the most simply produced. The only preparation required is to use thin unwired wax foundation in the comb frames. When the comb is removed from the hive it is cut to fit the containers available and is eaten complete with the wax.

Section honey is similar to cut comb except that wooden boxes called sections are put into the hive and the bees fill these with comb. The full boxes are then removed from the hive and wrapped.

Chapter 3

YOUR OPTIONS AND OBJECTIVES

WHY are you keeping or thinking about starting to keep bees ?

The answer to this question will have a bearing on the equipment you need and on the method you should use to manage your stocks of bees. It will help you to make the right decisions from the alternatives given in the following chapters.

This page will at least tell you about some of the options available to you.

Is your object to produce :
- Honey?
- Wax?
- Pollen?
- Propolis?
- Royal jelly?

Are you going to produce one or more of these for :
- Your own use?
- For sale to cover your costs?
- As a profitable enterprise?
- For showing in competitions?

Are you going to breed additional stocks:
- For your own use?
- For sale?

Do you have some other object in mind :
- Crop pollination?
- Breed improvement?
- Interesting hobby?

WHERE are you going to keep them?
- At home in the garden, on the garage roof
- At a remote site (out apiary)

Are you going to keep them at one fixed location, or move them between different crops of productive forage (migratory beekeeping)?

HOW MANY colonies are you going to start with and how many are you eventually going to have?

Chapter 4

GETTING STARTED

This chapter tells you about the essential specialist equipment you need to start beekeeping, how to chose the form you get your stock in and how to chose a type of hive.

▼ PROTECTIVE CLOTHING

Good bee-proof clothing gives you confidence. You can examine a colony of bees much more calmly if you are not continually worried about being stung. Calm and gentle handling helps to keep the bees quiet and makes the job much easier and pleasurable.

It is a good idea to get your protective clothing well before you get bees. This will let you go to practical beekeeping demonstrations and see the various operations carried out by experienced beekeepers.

Protective clothing is an area where you can improvise. The only specialised items you will want at first are a **VEIL** and (probably) **GLOVES.** More general items are a **HAT** which bees will not get caught up in, an **OVERALL** and a pair of **WELLINGTON BOOTS**.

White or light coloured clothing is preferable as this tends not to annoy the bees as much as dark, particularly dark blue, clothing. Light clothing is also cooler, remember you are usually going to be dressed up in all of this in hot weather. One exception to this rule is your veil. Black veils are much more easily seen through than white.

There is a wide selection of specialised protective clothing available and some examples are given in the chapter on equipment.

▼ THE BASIC TOOLS

There are two specialised tools that you will need, a **SMOKER** and a **HIVE TOOL**.

The **SMOKER** is used to "*subdue*" the bees by allowing you to introduce controlled quantities of smoke into the hives. The threat of impending fire, and the possible need to leave the hive makes them eat as much honey as possible. This becomes their prime objective keeps them busy while you examine the hive.

The smoker itself comprises a container with a spout and a pair of bellows. The container part holds smouldering fuel and the smoke is produced by using the bellows to drive air through the smouldering fuel.

The **HIVE TOOL** is used to separate the parts of the hive which have usually been stuck together with propolis. There are two types of hive tool commonly in use.

1   A flat steel blade about one and a half inches wide and nine inches long, bent up at one end with both ends sharpened.

2   A thicker steel blade with one end sharpened and with a hook at the other end (the J type).

The J type is particularly useful for levering out the frames of comb.

There are several different forms you can get your stock in:

1 A COLONY. This is a complete stock of bees on at least eleven frames of comb. A colony is usually purchased with its hive but is sometimes available "*with frames*" to put into your own hive.

With a full colony you will have a lot of bees about when you start to examine your stock.

The advantage of getting a complete colony is that you can get a crop of honey in your first season. There are two disadvantages, you will have a lot of bees about when you start to examine your stock and you will have to think about swarm control in your first season.

2   **A NUCLEUS STOCK.** This has a queen bred in the current season with four to six frames of comb and contains brood in all stages of development. A nucleus is normally purchased "*with frames*" which are transported in a nucleus box. A nucleus box is a thin walled, half width hive with a ventilated roof and a small entrance which can be closed up for transport.

The advantages of getting a nucleus are there are fewer bees about while you are learning and you will not normally have to worry about swarming in the first season. The disadvantage is that you are unlikely to get a honey crop in your first season.

3   **A SWARM.** This is a low cost or no cost way of getting stock depending on the number of swarms in the current season. A swarm is bees only, headed by a queen normally at least one year old. More detailed information on swarms is given in colony management.

Swarms, in particular swarms from an unknown source, should be hived on frames with wax foundation only, not on previously drawn comb. Some diseases of bees are transmitted in honey and the technique of hiving swarms on foundation means that they are not able to store any of the honey that they have brought with them but use it up while they are drawing fresh comb.

The advantage of starting with a swarm is cost. The disadvantages are that you are unlikely to get a honey crop in the first season and that you need to get a sample of the bees examined for disease.

A swarm is free

19

4 A PACKAGE. Packages comprise a young queen and a few hundred bees and are again "*bees only*". In the past this method was used to obtain queens which had been raised early in the season in warmer climates. This form of selling stock has almost disappeared as a result of UK import controls which are designed to prevent the spread of disease.

▼ CHOOSING A TYPE OF HIVE

The choice of type of hive is the area where you will get the greatest amount of conflicting advice. The main point to remember here is that all modern types are being used successfully so the choice is not as important as many will make out.

One important factor if you are going to have more than one hive is to stick to one type so that the parts are interchangeable.

The first decision is an easy one, that is the choice between **DOUBLE WALLED** and **SINGLE WALLED.**

The **DOUBLE** walled hive comprise thin walled brood boxes and supers with separate outer covers or **LIFTS** which leave a space between the inner and outer parts of the hive.

The advantages of the double walled hive are better weather protection and its traditional attractive appearance.

The double walled hive is the most attractive

The disadvantages are that it is difficult to transport, has twice as many parts to move when you are inspecting your stock, no flat roof to use as a temporary parking place for one of the parts of the hive while you are inspecting one of the other parts. Because of its good insulating properties, brood rearing may be slowed down in the spring and finally it is much more expensive.

The **SINGLE** walled hive comprises thick walled boxes with no outer cover. Single walled types of hive by far the most popular. In the UK the two most popular types are the **NATIONAL** and the **SMITH.**

Single walled hives are far more popular

The only practical difference between the national and smith hives is in the ease of handling. The frames hang from ledges at the top of each of the chambers of the hive. These ledges are wider in the **NATIONAL** hive allowing for longer **LUGS** at the top of each frame which makes them easier to handle. The chambers or **BOXES** of the national hive themselves are also more easily handled as the frame support ledges project to provide a "*handle*". The advantages of the **SMITH** hive are its lower cost and ease of construction.

Choosing Single or Double Brood Chamber

The advantages of a single brood chamber are:

1 Honey yield is higher (most professionals use single).
2 Fewer frames to examine when performing brood nest operations.
3 Upper chamber does not have to be removed to examine the lower chamber.

The advantages of a double brood chamber are:

1 The incidence of swarming is reduced with the larger brood nest.
2 Swarm control is easier, see Chapter 5.
3 Comb replacement in the spring is easier as the bees are not using all of them.

▼ CHOOSING A LOCATION FOR THE HIVES

The first decision is whether to keep them at home in the garden or to obtain a site for an out apiary.

The advantages of the home site are:

1 It is easier to make quick regular checks.
2 Your equipment is on hand.
3 You do not have transport problems.
4 Swarms are more readily detectable.

The disadvantages of a home site are:

1 It is difficult to work near the entrances in summer.
2 Neighbours are not always as enthusiastic as you.

The advantages of the out apiary are:

1 The bees can be near a good source of forage.
2 There can be more choice in the situation of the hives.

The hives should be in an airy but not exposed position

The Situation of The Hives

The following comments on hive situation are not mandatory. Many successful beekeepers have to disregard some of them. These conditions are given as a guide to avoiding future problems and should be considered when deciding which site to use.

For your own convenience the hive entrances should not face a path or other area which cannot be avoided during the active summer season.

To reduce the effect of dampness, the hives should be in an airy but not exposed position and should not have overhanging trees or cables which will drip water on them.

To assist the bees in locating their own hive, the hives should not be regimented in rows and columns but arranged randomly.

To assist the bees in locating their own hives they should be arranged randomly.

Chapter 5

COLONY MANAGEMENT

Colony management is about getting the bees to do what you want them to do. In most cases it is a matter of making use of their own natural reactions to get the result that you want. One example of getting the bees to do what you want is subduing with smoke as described in the last chapter.

There are a number factors that you are able to influence:

1 The strength of the colony i.e. the number of workers in it and the timing of an increase in strength.
2 Drifting of bees between colonies.
3 The location of the bees in relation to particular forage in order to get single source honey.
4 The behaviour of the colony while they are being examined.
5 Swarm control/queen rearing/making an increase.
6 Hiving a swarm by making use of the bees natural instincts.

▼ MANAGING THE COLONY STRENGTH

The most common reason for wanting to change the strength of a colony is to maximize the foraging force at the time of a nectar flow.

Increasing the Foraging Force by Feeding

The easiest way to increase the strength of the colony is to induce the queen to increase the rate at which she lays eggs. As the queens rate of egg laying depends on the amount of nectar coming into the hive, she can be induced to increase her egg laying rate by feeding the colony with weak sugar syrup. The sugar syrup is fed to the bees while they are in the hive.

There are three types of feeder available:

1 A vacumn feeder which is an inverted, airtight container with holes in the lid for the bees to feed through. The lid with holes is mounted over the opening in the cover board.
2 A container which provides access for the bees up through a central chamber or funnel and down to an outer syrup container.
3 A container which replaces a frame in the hive with access for bees at the top and with a perforated float for them to feed through.

For more details on feeders are given in the chapter on equipment.

Timing

Timing is of great importance when increasing the foraging force as a large stock before the forage is available will consume food rather than produce it.

As it takes 21 days from the queen laying an egg to the emergence of the worker bee and about another 21 days before that worker becomes a forager, you need to stimulate the queen to lay at least 6 weeks before the forage starts to yield.

Increasing the Foraging Force by Uniting

Each colony of bees is able to recognise the members of that colony by a colony odour. In order to unite two colonies you have to prevent them from mixing before they acquire a common odour.

There are two methods which can be used to achieve a common odour:

1 Separating the colonies with a sheet of newspaper which they chew their way through getting a common odour in the process.
2 Sprinkling sugar syrup over the bees of both colonies so that they acquire a common odour as they are cleaning each other up.

The first method is by far the most common. The brood chambers of the two colonies are placed on top of each other with a sheet of newspaper between them. A few pin holes can be made in the paper to give them a start. You must be careful in hot weather as the upper chamber will be "*bee tight*" and overheating can result. In this case you might need to provide ventilation (see the chapter on equipment). The resultant colony will end up with one queen. If you want it to be a particular one of the two original queens, you must remove the other one before you unite the two colonies. If you unite two colonies which both have queens, one of the queens will kill the other.

The newspaper method has the advantage of restricting the bees which have been moved to their new hive for a day or so. this results in them reorienting themselves when they fly out and helps to prevent them returning to their original site.

▼ DRIFTING OF BEES BETWEEN COLONIES

Every rule has its exception. Worker bees do not invariably return to their own hive. This fact is particularly noticeable when the returning bee is flying into a strong wind and her own hive is one of a straight row. The worker bee with a full load of nectar will be accepted by the colony whose hive she enters and this is often one of the first she comes to. Drifting is normally discouraged by placing hives in a random pattern rather than in straight lines and by making individual hives more recognizable to the bees.

▼ SELECTING FORAGE

The only certain method of securing specific honey crops is to practice migratory beekeeping i.e. to take them to an area where the only nectar yeilding plants in a three mile radius provide the type of forage you want e.g. on a heather moor. If you move them near to a high yeilding crop e.g. oil seed rape, they will almost certainly work that crop exclusively.

A colony of bees generates a surprising amount of heat. When hives are closed to be moved they need good ventilation to prevent melting the wax comb. See the information on Travelling Screens in the chapter on equipment.

▼ CONTROL DURING EXAMINATION

The use of smoke to control bees during a colony examination, has already been described.

Other natural reactions of the bees can be used, some of these are:

Their tendency to run uphill.
Their preference for the dark (covered) parts of the hive.
The fact that bees of nursing age will tend to cover brood.
The instinct to return to their original location.

The use of smoke to control bees during a colony examination

▼ SWARM AVOIDANCE/QUEEN REARING /MAKING AN INCREASE

Swarm avoidance, queen rearing and making an increase are related subjects.
An attempt to perform one of these functions, certainly at a simple level, results in (or depends on) at least one of the others occurring.You will see how they are related in the following text. Most of the information is given under the Swarm Avoidance heading.

To understand the various techniques which follow, you need to know a little about three subjects:

1 How a colony is able to produce a new queen.
2 The conditions which result in the colony starting to produce a new queen.
3 Swarming.

▼ HOW A COLONY PRODUCES A NEW QUEEN

Bees are able to produce a queen by feeding a larvae which has hatched from a fertile egg, i.e. a larvae which would have developed into a worker, on a special food known as **ROYAL JELLY.**   Royal jelly is fed for the whole five days of the larval stage of development.

The wax cell needed for the development of a queen is much larger than that needed for a worker, this cell is constructed vertically rather than horizontally. A normal worker cell can be extended outwards and downwards by the bees for this purpose.

The wax cell needed for the development of a queen is much larger and constructed vertically.

Alternatively special vertical **QUEEN CUPS** are constructed by the bees. After the queen has laid an egg in a queen cup it is extended downwards by the bees until it resembles an inverted acorn.

The extended cell is then known as a **QUEEN CELL**

Conditions for Queen Rearing

There are three situations which result in the colony setting about raising one or more queens.

1   When they are superseding the queen

When the queen's ability to lay eggs becomes impaired e.g. through old age, the bees produce "*supersedure*" queen cells. There are normally fewer of these than in swarming, often only one or two.

2   When brood and nurse bees are isolated from the queen.
Isolation can occur within the hive or remote from the hive.

2a When eggs and young larvae are separated from the brood nest

Bees tend to produce queen cells if eggs and/or young larvae are moved to a remote part of the hive e.g. above the honey storage supers. This is particularly likely if the queen does not have access to that part of the hive due to her restriction by the queen excluder.

Emergency queen cells are built on the face of the comb

2b When queenless bees have access to eggs or young larvae

The queen cells produced under these circumstances are known as *"emergency"* queen cells. It is possible that emergency queen cells result in inferior queens particularly if they are built over older larvae,but this is not as common as many people claim. Emergency queen cells are built on the face of the comb.

3 When they are preparing to swarm

Swarming

Swarming is a natural instinct of bees and is their method of propagating the species. There are a number of factors which contribute to the bees making swarm preparations. The most important factor is unavailability of laying space for the queen. This is one of the strongest arguments for using a double brood chamber. When the bees decide to swarm the queen lays eggs in a number of queen cups (usually 10 to 20).

When the queen cells are about to be sealed, that is nine days after the egg was laid, The old queen and a large proportion of the colony leave the hive in a swarm and set about finding a new home. They usually congregate a few yards from the hive while *"scouts"* go out to look for a suitable new location.

If a double brood chamber is used there is a vertical space available between the frames of the two boxes. The *"swarming"* queen cells are almost always on the bottom of the frames of the upper box.

Swarming queen cells are almost always on the bottom of the frames of the upper box.

▼ SWARM AVOIDANCE

One of the most important aspects of beekeeping is the avoidance of swarms. This is because a swarm leaves the colony with a depleted stock and, more significantly without a laying queen for the best part of a month. The stock is therefore depleted for the remainder of the season and the honey surplus, if there is one at all, will be small. One thing to remember when deciding on one of the following methods of swarm avoidance is that you need the largest possible foraging force to gather a honey surplus. One large colony will produce much more honey than the same number of bees spread over two colonies.

It is very easy to prevent bees swarming at a cost of your honey crop. You need a good method of swarm avoidance to get a balance between yield and incidence of swarming.

▼ SWARM PREVENTION OR SWARM CONTROL

You have a choice of technique in your attempt to not allow the bees to swarm.

You can try to prevent the occurence of the conditions for swarming. Techniques which use this premise are known as **SWARM PREVENTION**.

You can regularly check your colonies and take some action when you discover swarm preparations.

Techniques which use this method are known as **SWARM CONTROL**.

Most of the techniques of prevention and control are based on a system devised in the USA in the 1880's by Demaree. The basic technique is known the Demaree method.

29

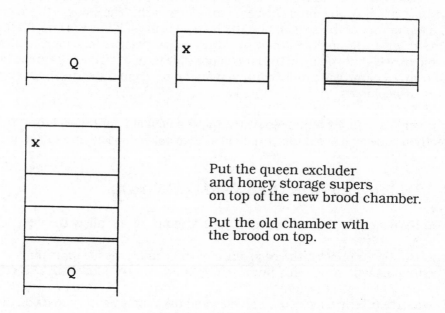

Super

Super
Queen Excluder

x

Brood Chamber
Floor

Move the hive aside
and put a floor and
empty brood chamber
at the original location.

x

Move the honey storage supers aside

x
Q

Find the queen and move the rest of the frame with the queen to the empty brood chamber with frames of foundation or empty drawn comb. Fill the space in the original brood chamber with a frame of foundation.

Q

x

x

Put the queen excluder
and honey storage supers
on top of the new brood chamber.

Put the old chamber with
the brood on top.

Q

Swarm prevention - the basic technique (Demaree method)

30

▼ SWARM PREVENTION

Most methods of swarm prevention result in a reduced honey crop but the compensation in ease of mind and lack of complaints may well make these methods attractive.

The swarm prevention techniques rely on a drastic reduction of the brood nest conjestion. There are many variations of the basic Demaree technique. The only factor which makes them prevention rather than control is the fact that they are performed before swarm preparations have started.

The first method to use when trying to find the queen is to use as little smoke as possible and look on the frames containing eggs, i.e. the frames where the queen is currently laying and where she is most likely to be.

Smoking at the entrance causes the queen to move upwards. If two **brood** chambers are being used, the upper one can be moved aside and is then the most likely place to find the queen.

Minimizing Numbers To Help in Finding the Queen

One of the natural instincts of the bee is to return to its home location. You can make use of this factor to change the colony strength. When you need to **FIND THE QUEEN** you can decrease the strength on a temporary basis to make it easier to find her.

Move the brood box aside and put just the honey storage supers on the hive floor at the original location.

Check that the queen is not on the underside of the queen excluder.

Put the queen excluder on top of the supers, put the brood box on top of the queen excluder and drive some of the bees down through the queen excluder into the supers with smoke.

This will reduce the number of bees in the brood box which will still contain the queen as she cannot go through the queen excluder.

Move the brood box aside again.

The returning foragers will go to the original location and into the supers they will not add to the number of bees in the brood box.

Finding the Queen, the last resort

If all attempts to find the queen fail and it is essential to find her e.g. if you are requeening because the old queen has become a drone layer, there is a drastic but foolproof method available.

The technique is to trap the queen under a queen excluder in an empty brood chamber. This is achieved by "running in" all of the bees in the brood nest and allowing the workers to go up through the excluder to the brood which has been replaced above the excluder.

The returning foraging bees will also go up through the excluder to the returned honey storage supers.

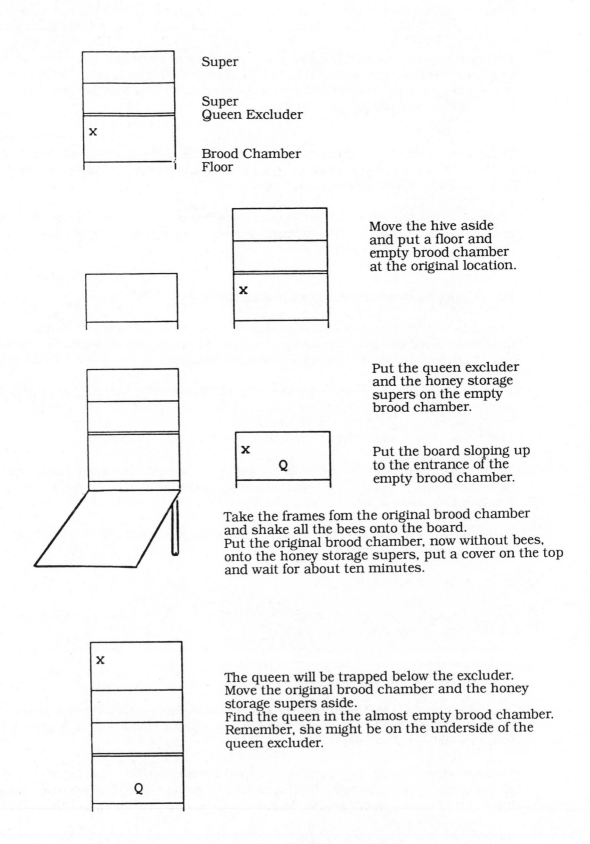

Super

Super
Queen Excluder

Brood Chamber
Floor

Move the hive aside
and put a floor and
empty brood chamber
at the original location.

Put the queen excluder
and the honey storage
supers on the empty
brood chamber.

Put the board sloping up
to the entrance of the
empty brood chamber.

Take the frames fom the original brood chamber
and shake all the bees onto the board.
Put the original brood chamber, now without bees,
onto the honey storage supers, put a cover on the top
and wait for about ten minutes.

The queen will be trapped below the excluder.
Move the original brood chamber and the honey
storage supers aside.
Find the queen in the almost empty brood chamber.
Remember, she might be on the underside of the
queen excluder.

Finding the queen, the last resort.

▼ SWARM CONTROL

Checking for Swarm Preparations.

The best techniques of swarm control i.e. those which are most likely to result in no swarming and a honey surplus, rely on a periodic check of the colony to see if they are preparing to swarm.

The five facts to remember here are:

1 The time between the queen laying an egg in a queen cup and the queen cell being sealed is nine days.
2 The swarm with the old queen leaves the hive as soon as suitable weather conditions allow after the first queen cell(s) have been sealed.
3 If a double brood chamber is used, the queen cells are normally constructed by the bees in the space between them.
4 Swarming normally occurs between the beginning of May and the end of August.
5 Drones must be present for swarming to occur.

The quickest and easiest way to check for swarm preparations is therefore to look between the upper and lower brood boxes at intervals of **NINE DAYS** or less from May until August and check that any queen cups/cells there do not contain eggs/larvae.

If there are no cups with eggs, they will not swarm in the next 9 days.
If there are no queen cells with lavae they will not swarm in the next 6 days.

If a double brood chamber is being used, the easiest way to make this inspection is to remove the supers, slide the upper brood box backwards and lift the back up with the front edge resting on the lower brood box as shown in the diagram.

If a single brood chamber is being used, it will be necessary to remove each frame from the brood nest to check for the presence of queen cells.

▼ REDUCING THE FREQUENCY OF INSPECTION

Swarming can be delayed by the practice of clipping the queens wings so that she is unable to fly.

As the queen cannot fly, the swarm cannot leave with the old queen 9 days after the start of swarm preparations.

The first swarm will be with a virgin queen which has taken 16 days to develop.

The frequency of inspection can therefore be reduced.

WARNING - Swarms headed by virgin queens often fly off quickly and do not normally cluster near the parent hive for very long. They are more easily lost.

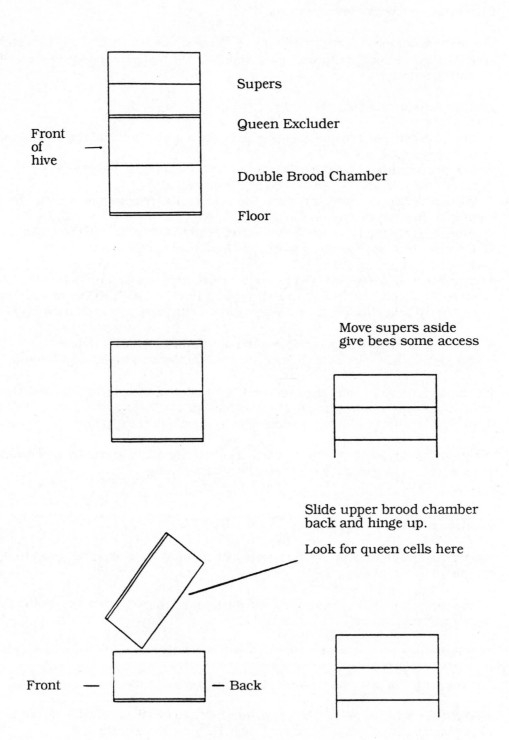

Supers

Queen Excluder

Front
of
hive

Double Brood Chamber

Floor

Move supers aside
give bees some access

Slide upper brood chamber
back and hinge up.

Look for queen cells here

Front — — Back

Checking for swarm preparations.

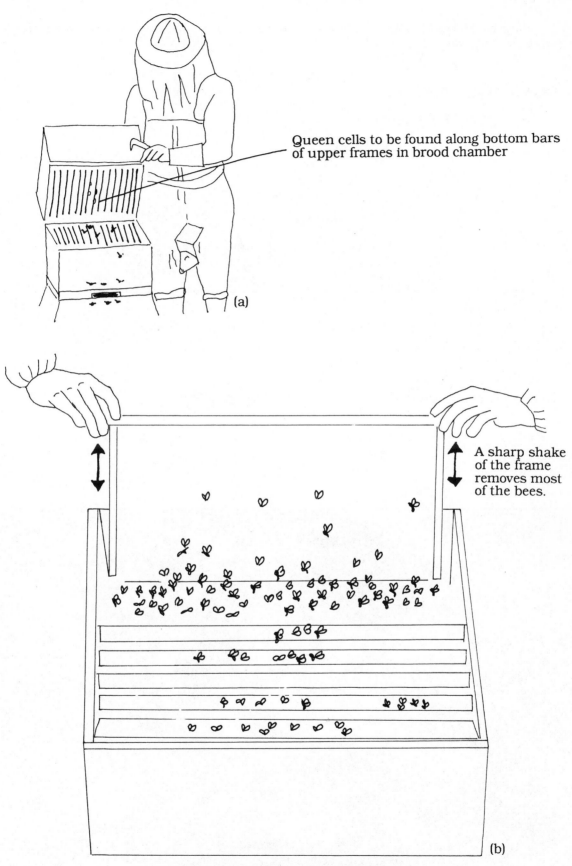

Queen cells to be found along bottom bars of upper frames in brood chamber

(a)

A sharp shake of the frame removes most of the bees.

(b)

Inspecting for queen cells.
(a) With double brood chamber system.
(b) With single brood chamber.

The diagram shows the latest stage you must detect to ensure that there will not be a swarm before your next inspection.

Days to next inspection

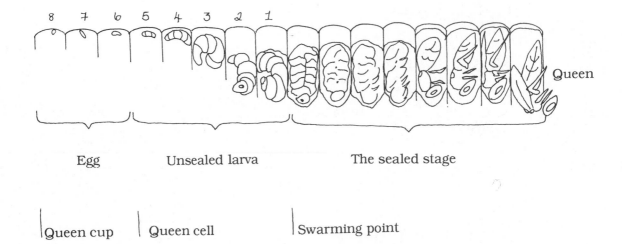

Egg   Unsealed larva   The sealed stage

Queen cup   Queen cell   Swarming point

With a single brood chamber you need to remove each frame.

▼ TO INCREASE OR NOT TO INCREASE ?

Almost all methods of swarm control will result in rearing a new queen.

You can therefore chose whether to make an increase in your number of colonies or not.

If you want to make an increase you will have a new queen to head your new colony.

If you do not want to make an increase, you can wait until the new queen is laying well, remove the old queen from the parent colony and unite.

▼ SWARM CONTROL OPTIONS

If the colonies have sufficient room for the queen to keep laying, then on average only one colony in three will make swarm preparations in any one year. The other two colonies will not need swarm control.

The most logical approach is therefore to check each colony for swarm preparations at seven to nine day intervals and practise swarm control only on the colonies which need it.

If you are not going to be able to make regular inspections, you will need to take measures which will almost certainly reduce your honey crop.

Remember that in these circumstances you will be practising swarm prevention on some colonies which would not have swarmed anyway.

Even if the method you need to use results in loss of honey crop you should still practise some form of swarm avoidance. Swarms are not only a disadvantage to the beekeeper, they are an unnecessary nuisance to the general public.

▼ MAKING AN ARTIFICIAL SWARM

Most of the successful swarm control techniques are variations of a basic technique known as making an artificial swarm.

The complete procedure for swarm control by making a basic artificial swarm is given here.

You will need a spare floor, brood chamber, cover board and roof.

You will also need eleven frames fitted with foundation.

Perform regular inspections until you find swarming preparations in progress.

The hive parts will already be separated for the inspection. Move the brood chamber(s) to a new location about two or three feet from the original site.

Set up the spare floor and brood chamber at the original location and put some of the new frames fitted with foundation (say five) into it. The returning flying bees will go into this new hive.

Now for the most difficult part. Examine the frames of the original brood chamber to find the queen.

When you have a frame with the queen on, put it into the new hive with the frames of foundation. Add another frame to get some young bees into this artificial swarm.

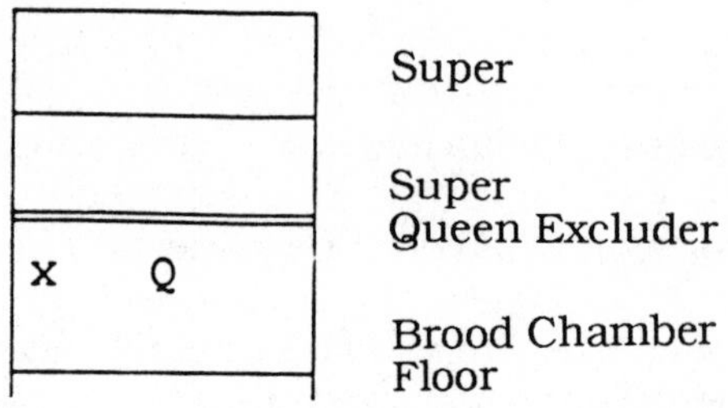

Super

Super
Queen Excluder

Brood Chamber
Floor

Move hive to one side and put new broodchamber on original site.

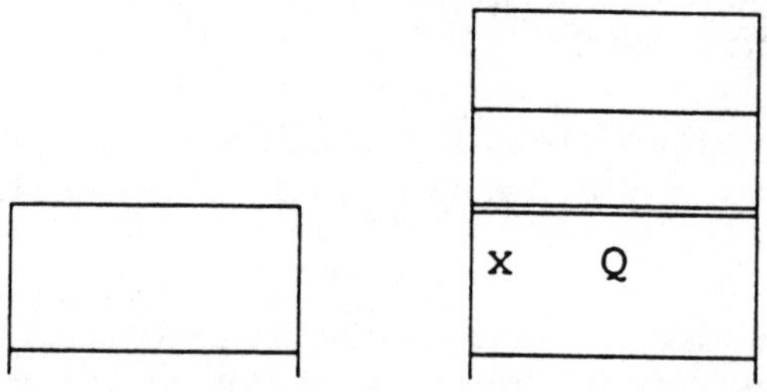

Remove supers and find the queen. Move the frame with the queen on and one other frame into the new brood chamber.
Fill the new brood chamber with frames of comb or foundation.

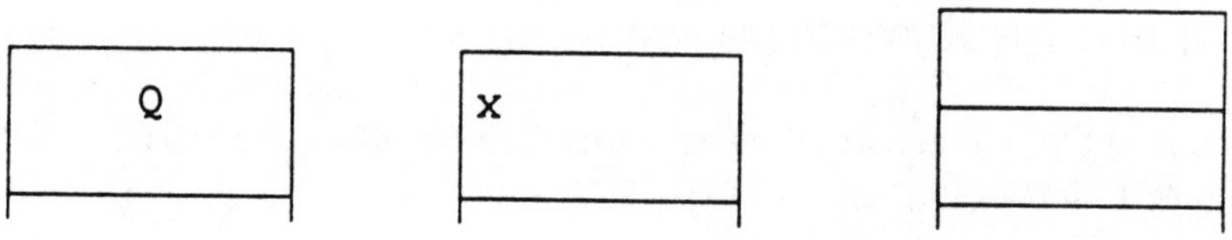

Put the queen excluder and supers on the artificial swarm.
Replace the two frames taken from the old brood chamber with frames of comb or foundation.

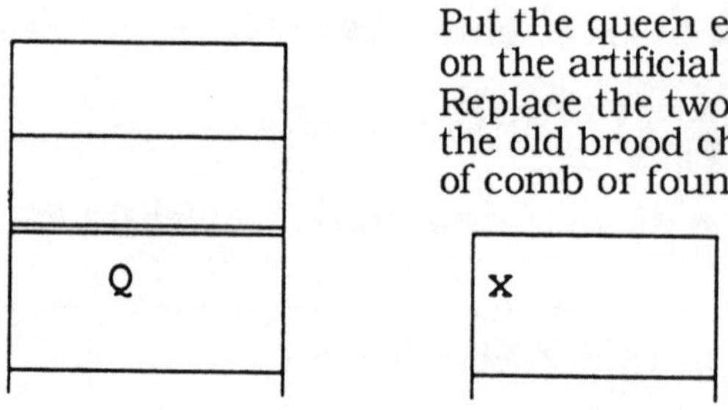

x = Old Brood Chamber
Q = Queen

Making an artificial swarm

Fill the new brood chamber with frames of foundation. this will leave you two frames of foundation to replace the frames removed from the original hive.

Put the supers if any on the artificial swarm at the old location.

Examine the frames of the original hive and cut out all except one queen cell. If possible leave one which is not yet sealed so that you can check that it contains a larvae. Handle this frame gently to avoid damage to the *"potential"* queen.

The artificial swarm with the old queen will not have brood to look after and will concentrate on drawing comb in the brood chamber and on filling the supers with honey.

Almost all of the flying bees will join the artificial swarm on the original location.

When the new queen in the original hive is mated and laying you have the choice of making an increase or removing the old queen and uniting.

▼ SIMPLE BUT NOT PREFERRED METHODS

There are three simple methods of swarm avoidance, they all have serious disadvantages in terms of yield but are sometimes useful in an emergency.

1 Remove the queen. The colony will produce emergency queen cells. Destroy all but one of the emergency queen cells eight days later.

The disadvantage of this method is about one months loss of brood rearing.

2 Split the colony into two. With this method you remove half of the combs from the brood nest and put them in another hive filling the remainder of both brood nests with frames of foundation. Each of the two halves of the original stock should be given half of the sealed stores and both should have eggs or young lavae. Two or three days later you look to see which of them has produced emergency queen cells and cut out all except one. After making sure that they have sufficient stores of food, you put any supers on the other colony i.e. the one with the original queen. This may give you a small honey surplus.

3 Remove four frames of eggs brood and stores to make up a nucleus and replace them with four frames of foundation. Similar to the previous method but with an uneven split. You need to check that the queen does not go into the nucleus and you need to shake in several more frames' worth bees.

This last method may only postpone swarming.

▼ EMERGENCY SWARM PREVENTION

If you suddenly need to leave your bees for a few weeks, there are some measures which you can take which will help to reduce swarming.

You should give plenty of honey storage space anyway, but adding an extra super helps avoid brood nest congestion.

An even greater aid is to add an extra brood chamber filled with frames of drawn comb or foundation.

▼ DEALING WITH A SWARM

Sooner or later you will have to deal with a swarm which may or may not be from one of your own colonies.

A swarm usually settles close (ten to a hundred yards) from its original hive. It usually stays there for several hours while scout bees are looking for a suitable new home. When it flies from the first settling point it may stop and re-cluster to give the queen, who is not built for distance flying, a rest.

The first stage of dealing with the swarm when you have located it is to get it into a container. The container can be a straw skep, a cardboard box or the hive that you are going to keep it in. The thing to remember if you are going to have to take the swarm any distance is to use a container which is portable.

The first stage is to get the swarm into a container or skep.

You can make use of three of the bees natural reactions when getting them into the container.

1 The swarm will cluster where the queen is.
2 They will tend to move upwards, both from their initial position and, when they are in the container, to the top of the container.
3 They will *"call"* the bees which have not yet joined the new cluster in the container by using scent organs.

40

The method of getting a large number of bees into the container varies according to their location.

If they are on a thin branch which can be cut off, you can hold the branch steady while you are cutting it, shake it firmly once over the container, and invert the container over or near to the branch. Put a wedge under the edge of the container to provide a good entrance.

If the branch cannot be cut, hold the container underneath the cluster and either give the branch one good shake or brush as many as possible into the container with your hand and invert the container. Remember to provide a good entrance as above.

The swarm may be on a fence post

If they are on a fence post you may be able invert your container over it. The bees can then be driven up into the container with a little smoke. Alternatively you may be able to brush a sufficient number into the container and invert it as before.

If there is no way to get them into a container, put one or more frames of comb which have previously held brood near and preferably above them. If necessary use a little smoke to start them moving onto these frames. They will re-cluster on the frames which can then be put directly into their new hive.

The bees will start to mark the location of your container by sticking their abdomens in the air (this exposes their scent glands) and fanning their wings. At this stage there will probably still be quite a few bees where they first settled. Use smoke to make these bees fly, they will be attracted by the scent of the calling bees and move into your container.

Leave the swarm in the container, near to where you found them until evening to let all the bees join the cluster.

▼ HIVING THE SWARM

If you did not use the new hive as a container to collect the swarm in, set one up where you are going to keep it. You will need a floor, deep brood chamber, eleven frames fitted with foundation, a cover board and a roof. Foundation is preferable to drawn comb as the bees will use any honey they have brought with them to draw new comb. If you use drawn comb they may store some of this honey which could carry the spores of the disease *"foul brood"*. If any robbing takes place before you get the results of a health check on the swarm you could infect nearby colonies with foul brood. Put a wide board from the ground up to the entrance of the new hive.

In the evening when the bees have stopped flying go and collect the swarm. Make sure that the container is bee-tight. One good method is to wrap it in a sheet.

Hold the container, open end down, over the board leading up to the hive entrance and give it one good shake to dislodge the bees and let them fall onto the board. Put the container down beside the board to let the remaining bees join those on the board. The natural instinct of the bees is to move upwards and they will go up the board and into the hive.

They may need a little smoke to get them moving and to move any bees from under the board or under the hive floor. You may well need to use some smoke to move the remaining bees out of the container.

The next day take a sample of bees and send them off for a health check.

They will go up the board and into the hive.

42

▼ QUEEN REARING

There are many techniques for queen rearing described in the specialist books. The one method given here is a simple one suitable for queen rearing on a very small scale.

The Preferred method of swarm control, making an artificial swarm, has already been described. The artificial swarm method produced a new queen so you already know how to produce a queen if the colony is making swarm preparations.

If your object is to produce one or more new queens you can induce the colony to make swarm preparations.

Remember

The main cause of swarming was the lack of space for the queen to lay eggs.
The queen can be stimulated to lay eggs by stimulative feeding.

The simplest method of queen rearing is therefore:

1 Restrict the brood nest to **ONE** brood chamber (or less with the use of **DUMMY BOARDS**). Dummy boards are solid frames which can be used to fill part of the brood nest.
2 Feed sugar syrup to the bees as fast as they will take it. This will both stimulate the queen to lay and help to fill the brood nest.
3 Carry out a check for swarm preparations at frequent (less than nine day) intervals.
4 When swarm preparations are found (queen cells present) make an artificial swarm.
5 Divide the original (parent) colony into one or two nucleus stocks with one good queen cell in each.

6 Make sure that each has at least one frame full of stored honey.

7 Check the nucleus stocks in 3 to 4 weeks for a laying queen.

Remember that the queen will need good weather for her mating flight(s). Bad weather can extend these times.

Chapter 6

COLONY PROTECTION

The colony needs protection from:

1 The Elements
2 Enemies (e.g. mice and wasps)
3 Its Own Internally Generated Heat when confined to the hive
4 Crop Spraying
5 Starvation, particularly in winter/spring

▼ PROTECTION FROM THE ELEMENTS

The greatest danger to bees, particularly in winter, is dampness. The hive should have a good, waterproof roof and be situated such that it has minimum exposure to driving rain while allowing a drying air flow. The hive should be slightly tilted forwards to prevent water running in.

Excessive wind causes problems for the flying bees. Some protection from high wind is advisable.

The best protection from driving rain and high wind while still allowing some air flow is a hedge or shrubbery. This has the added advantage that it prevents low flying by the bees which can cause nuisance.

In winter there can be two cases where bees need protection.

1 Snow on its own usually allows a sufficient passage of air for the bees survival. Air is normally available through a vent in the cover board as well as the entrance.

If the snow melts and water on the front of the hive freezes, the entrance can be blocked with ice. In this case a vent in the cover board is necessary to provide an air supply.

2 The reflection of the sun on snow can cause a bright light at the hive entrance. This light will attract the bees out where there is a high probability of their being chilled and unable to fly back to the hive. The solution to this problem is to lean a board against the front of the hive to shield the entrance from the glare.

▼ PROTECTION FROM ENEMIES

The two main enemies that bees need protection from are mice and wasps

Mice are a problem in the winter when the bees are clustered and are in a lethargic state. At that time the mice are able to enter the hive without being chased out by the bees. The mice eat the comb and the bees will move off onto other combs until they are restricted to a part of the hive which may not have sufficient stores. A wire mesh which will allow the passage of bees but not mice, known as a mouse guard, is fitted over the entrance in the autumn and left there until the spring.

In late summer, wasps try to enter the hive to steal honey. The bees attack the wasps to defend their stores. The bees sting is barbed and each bee that stings dies. The wasp sting is not barbed and it is therefore able to kill many bees.

To help the bees defend the hive against attack by wasps, the size of the entrance can be reduced with an entrance block. An entrance block is a piece of wood which fits into the normal entrance. The entrance block has a small, easily defendable, entrance cut into it.

Other bees may try to steal the stores of a weak colony. Robbing can be minimised by using an entrance block.

Hives sometimes need protection from disturbance by other livestock e.g. sheep, goats, or cows. Where such protection is necessary the hives should be enclosed with suitable fencing.

Another danger is from vandals. Protection in this case must be achieved by suitable location of the hives.

Special cases may be encountered in a particular locality e.g. damage to the hive by woodpeckers. Some of these cases are covered in the specialist literature but in general you will have to devise your own solution or seek the advice of other local beekeepers.

▼ PROTECTING CONFINED COLONIES FROM THEIR OWN INTERNALLY GENERATED HEAT

A colony may be confined to the hive for a number of reasons e.g. in preparation for and during moving, or for protection from crop spraying.

A colony normally produces a great deal of heat to maintain the temperature of the brood nest and to facilitate wax comb production.

When the hive entrance is open, surplus heat is dispersed by the bees creating an air circulation current. They achieve this by fanning with their wings on one side of the hive entrance.

If the bees are to be confined to the hive they must be given adequate ventilation. The roof should be removed or raised and the cover board should be replaced with a travelling screen. A travelling screen is a framed bee proof mesh. The entrance closure can be a type of spray entrance (see protection from crop spraying) instead of an air tight closure and, depending on the ambient temperature, a ventilator could be fitted in the hive floor.

Further information is given in Chapter 7 Equipment (Equipment for confining/moving bees).

▼ PROTECTION FROM CROP SPRAYING

Large numbers of bees can be killed if they are caught in crop sprays. If the co-operation of local farmers can be obtained to notify you when crop spraying is going to take place, you can confine the bees to their hive during the day of the spraying operation.

A spray entrance, which allows bees to enter the hive but not leave it, should be fitted on the evening before spraying is to take place. It is even more important than normal to provide a source of water for the bees after the spraying has taken place as they might otherwise use the sprayed chemical as a water source.

Protecting the bees from the crop spray by confining them to their hive will mean that you will also have to protect them from excessive heat which will be generated by a confined colony.

This can be achieved by using a travelling screen and possibly by using a ventilated floor.

▼ PROTECTION FROM STARVATION

There are two conditions which can lead to colony starvation:

1 All of the stores being used when there is no nectar flow.
2 A gap in the stores which the winter cluster of bees is unable to cross because of low temperature. This is known as isolation starvation.

If sufficient honey (30 to 50lbs) is left in the hive in the autumn and the bees are given an autumn feed of sugar syrup, it is only necessary to check that they have stores left about once a month during the winter. The usage of stores depends mainly on temperature, minimum usage being at about freezing point.

In the early spring when brood is being raised and the nectar flow has not started A high usage of stores occurs and more frequent checking is required. If the stores are depleted the type of feeding required depends on the temperature. At low temperatures a soft candy can be fed. At higher temperatures liquid sugar syrup can be fed.

The bees store their winter supply at top of the hive and work their way up through it. If they work up through the centre and then move to one side, they may not be able to cross the gap to the other side because of low temperature. In this case a bridge of candy will provide a food supply which they can use while working their way across the hive.

▼ PROTECTION FROM DISEASE

Protect from foul brood by not giving the bees access to honey, particularly honey from an unknown source. This is the reason for hiving stray swarms on foundation. They use up the honey that they have brought with them for comb drawing and store fresh supplies.

Have the health of bees from an unknown source checked before they have time to drift into other hives.

Chapter 7

EQUIPMENT

This chapter tells you about equipment under the following headings:

1 Protective Clothing
2 Tools
3 Hives
4 Frames and Foundation
5 Feeders
6 Equipment for Confining/Moving Bees
7 Equipment for Harvesting the Honey Crop
8 Equipment for Processing the Honey Crop
9 Equipment for Other Hive Products
10 Equipment for Colony Protection
11 Miscellaneous Equipment (queen marking, clipping)

The basics of the first four items in the list above have been covered in earlier chapters. This chapter deals with equipment in a little more detail but is not exhaustive. The equipment manufacturers and suppliers' catalogues are a useful source of information on this subject.

Good protective clothing is essential for confidence.

▼ PROTECTIVE CLOTHING

The most important items of protective clothing are those which protect your face and in particular your eyes.

Hats

There are several types of hat available specifically designed for beekeepers to wear with a veil. The special hats usually have some form of bee proof ventilation to make them more comfortable to wear in hot weather. In general the types of hat available are: Mesh Helmets, Polythene Helmets, and Cloth Hats. All have rims to hold the veil away from your face.

Veils

The Veils available range from simple net veils with elastic at the end which fits over your hat, to a folding, net covered frame with a zip to fit it to a suit of overalls. Between these options are veils with cloth "*bibs*" front and back which can be tied round your chest, and veils with large rings to hold them away from your face.

Combined Hat and Veil

The combined hat and veil is normally a cloth hat with a ring veil fixed to either a stiff or foldable brim.

Gloves

Beekeeping gloves comprise a pair of sting-proof gloves with elasticated gauntlets. The type which is the least difficult to work in are made of soft thin leather, these are of course the most expensive. Cheaper alternatives are made from canvas and plastic. Rubber "*washing up*" gloves with elastic bands round the forearms, are suitable if you are able to work in them.

Bee Suits

Bee suits are either jacket or complete overall types. Both types are fitted with a hood which has a framed veil at the front. The hood is often zipped on for ease of use and the hood may be a stiff type which allows air circulation round your head to keep you cool.

Bee suits should not have "*through pockets*" as in normal overalls. If you are adapting a normal pair of overalls, be sure to sew up the "*through pockets*" to keep the bees outside.

▼ TOOLS

The tools described here are those used in colony manipulation. The tools used for making up hive parts and frames are covered in the relevant appendices.

Smokers

Smokers vary in size, material of construction, and method of producing the air flow.

The most popular smoker is a 7 inch by 3 inch copper smoker with bellows.

Sizes vary from 7 to 10 inches high and 3 to 4 inches diameter.

Construction materials used are: Copper, stainless steel, Tin plated steel and enamelled steel.

The air flow is produced by manual bellows or a fan. The fan may be clockwork or battery powered.

The most popular smoker is a 7 inch by 3 inch copper smoker with bellows.

Fuel suitable for use in smokers should burn slowly and produce a cool smoke. Two of the most popular fuels are: rolls of corrugated cardboard and hessian sacking. When using hessian from old sacks make sure that the sack did not previously contain insecticide.

Hive Tools

There are two basic designs of hive tool, The flat blade bent up at one end, usually known as the standard hive tool and the J type, as described in the getting started chapter.

There are variations in size and strength of these two types.

▼ HIVES

There are many variations of the basic hive in use throughout the world. These have generally been developed to be most efficient for local conditions.

It is advisable to choose a type which is in common use locally because:

1 It is more likely to be suitable for your conditions
2 Hive parts, suitable frames and foundation will be more readily available
3 Nucleus stocks will be available on the correct frames.
4 You can produce saleable nucleus stocks on suitable frames.

The basic hive parts and advantages/disadvantages of the different types of hive were covered in Chapters 2 and 4.

There are a few hive parts available for special purposes.

The Section Crate

The section crate is a special form of super which is designed to hold the wooden section boxes for the production of section honey. The section crate fits on the hive in the same way as a super, it has a slatted base to support the section boxes and its height is the same height as a section box.

The Heather Floor

The heather floor is a ventilated floor with a built in entrance closing mechanism. this type of floor is designed with migratory beekeeping in mind and is used for colonies which are going to be moved to both heather and other forage.

Swarm Control Boards

Swarm control boards are special cover boards with small closable entrances on three sides and usually with bee proof mesh in the center. These control boards are used in swarm control techniques when the parent colony is located over the artificial swarm.

▼ FRAMES AND FOUNDATION

Nothing seems to cause more confusion to new beekeepers than the assortment of frames available and the correct selection of frame types. This is partly due to the way in which manufacturers specify them. They are really quite easy to select.

The frames described here are those suitable for the types of hive commonly used in the UK (National, Smith and WBC). Each of these types of hive uses frames which are fitted with British Standard (BS) wax foundation.

Frames have three components: One top bar
                                         Two side bars
                                         Two bottom bars

The Top Bar

There are two variables relating to the top bar which you need to specify. The choices depend on the type of hive that they are going to be used in and whether they are going to be used in the brood chamber or in the supers.

1 Long or short lugs. The lugs are the extension of the top bar beyond the side frame.

National and WBC hives need long lugs (top bar length 17 inches).
Smith hives need short lugs (top bar length 15 1/2 inches).

2 Wide or narrow tops. Wide and narrow refer to the width of the part of the top bar between the side bars.

Wide (1 1/16 inches) top bars are usually used in the brood nest.
Narrow (7/8 inch) top bars are usually used in the supers.

The Side Bars

The choice of side bars depends on whether they are going to be used in a deep or shallow box and on the method you are going to use for frame spacing. the choices are:

1 Deep or shallow
2 Straight-narrow, Self spacing (Hoffman), Straight-wide (Manley)

Frames made with the straight-narrow side bars need spacers to correctly space them in the hive. The spacers can be metal or plastic spacers which fit over the frame lugs, or castellated metal strips which fit in the hive. The use of this type of side bar allows different spacing by selection of spacers.

The self spacing (Hoffman) side bars are the most commonly used. The side bar is shaped to minimize the area of contact between frames. The small contact area makes it easier to separate the frames when the bees have propolised them together.

The straight-wide (Manley) side bars are often used for the production of cut comb honey because the comb surface is usually flatter and the comb is often drawn out further. Another advantage of this type is that the edges of the wide top bar and stepped bottom bar can be used as a knife guide when uncapping. If you are going to extract honey from the frames it is advisable to check that your extractor will accept the wider Manley frames before you choose them.

The Bottom Bars

The choice of bottom bar is generally governed by your previous choice of top and side bars.

There are two types of bottom bar:

1 The straight-narrow type
2 The stepped type

The straight type is the normal bottom bar.

The stepped type is usually used with the straight-wide Manley side bars.
Some beekeepers prefer to use the stepped type in conjunction with wide top bars in brood chambers as they are believed to discourage the building of brace comb.

The Hanging Section Frame

The hanging section frame is a wooden frame which holds three wooden section boxes, each of which is fitted with a square of wax foundation. The hanging section frame is used in a normal super with ordinary frames. It has two advantages over a section crate: The bees go into it to start drawing the comb more readily, and if you want to produce just a few sections you do not have to produce a full crate.

Foundation

The bees are persuaded to build their combs in the frames by fitting the frames with sheets of wax which are impressed with the shape of the cells. These sheets of wax are known as foundation.

There are two sizes commonly available in Britain, one for deep frames and one for shallow frames. They are suitable for the frames which fit National, Smith and WBC hives as the inside dimensions of these frames are the same.

The sheets of foundation are available with wire embedded in them for additional strength. The strengthening wire helps to hold the comb in the frame both when it is being examined in the apiary and when honey is being extracted in a centrifugal extractor.

Unwired foundation is also available and this is mainly used for cut comb honey production.

Individual squares of foundation are used in the wooden section boxes.

Other sizes for different hives are listed in the equipment manufacturers catalogues.

▼ FEEDERS

The liquid feed for bees is known as sugar syrup. Sugar syrup is made by putting sugar in a container and noting the level. As hot water is added the level will fall, continue to add hot water until the original level has been reached. Stir well, allow to cool to about 100 degrees Fahrenheit, and stir again.

There are three types of feeder in common use for feeding bees with sugar syrup:

1 The pail type
2 The Miller type and its variations
3 The frame type

Pail Feeders

Pail feeders comprise a container with a perforated, but otherwise airtight, lid. This container is filled with sugar syrup and inverted. A little syrup comes out of the perforations in the lid and then the vacuum holds the rest in. The feeder is placed in this state over the hole in the cover board and the bees suck the syrup down out of it.

Miller Type Feeders

The Miller feeder is the best known of a type which rely on the same general principle. This type of feeder comprises a container which has a central chamber, open at the top and bottom and reaching up to about 1/2 inch from the top. this central chamber is covered with an inverted U shaped part which extends from the top to about 1/8 inch from the bottom. The outer container is filled with sugar syrup which flows into the space between the inverted U shaped part and the central chamber. The complete feeder is placed such that the bees have access through the feed hole in the cover board into the central chamber, up through the central chamber, over the top and down into the space between the outside of the central chamber and the inside of the inverted U part.

Frame Feeders

The frame feeder is an open topped box, the same size and shape as a frame which hangs in the hive in place of one of the normal frames. The box contains a perforated, platform which floats on the top of the sugar syrup. The bees enter from the open top and have access to the syrup through the holes in the float.

▼ EQUIPMENT FOR CONFINING/MOVING BEES

You may need to confine bees to their hive:

1 To move them
2 To protect them e.g. from crop spraying

A colony of bees produces a large amount of heat and if they are confined without adequate ventilation the wax combs will melt in a very short time. The minimum ventilation required can be provided with a bee proof perforated cover (see Travelling Screen below). A ventilated floor should also be considered if the ambient temperature is likely to be high during the time that the bees are confined.

If the colony is being confined in order to be moved, the moveable parts must be securely fixed together. The most amusing (afterwards) stories about beekeeping usually result from a failure to adequately secure hives before moving them.

The Travelling Screen

The travelling screen comprise a bee proof mesh on a frame which fits on the top of the hive in place of the cover board. The travelling screen provides adequate ventilation for a confined colony under most circumstances. The roof must either be left off or must be raised to allow ventilation, in order to make the travelling screen effective when the bees are confined.

Ventilated Floors

Floors are available with bee proof ventilators in them to supplement the effect of the travelling screen under conditions of higher ambient temperature. Normal Floors can be easily adapted to provide bee proof ventilation.

The travelling screen provides adequate ventilation.

The Spray Entrance

The spray entrance is a device which allows the passage of bees in one direction only, into the hive. It is used when there is a requirement to get all of the bees into the hive before confining them e.g. before crop spraying takes place. The spray entrance comprises a row of lightweight vertical "*fingers*" which are longer than the depth of the entrance and therefore lie at an angle. When returning bees enter the hive they push their way in, lifting the "*fingers*" which drop back into place. Because fingers are angled inward the bees are not able to push their way out.

▼ EQUIPMENT FOR SECURING HIVES

There are a number of devices available for securing the movable parts of hives together in order to be able to move them safely.

1 Staples
2 Lock Slides
3 Straps

Short Metal Staples

Metal staples are cheap and effective but not popular as they damage the hive. An alternative method of using strips of wood nailed down each of the four sides presents the same problem of damaging the hive and will eventually result in an overall higher cost than using a more expensive fixing which will not damage the hive.

Lock Slides

Lock slides comprise two brackets, one for each movable chamber, into which a shaped wedge is tapped to fix the two chambers together. Lock slides need to be fitted to only the two opposite sides of each chamber, they do however need to be fixed fairly accurately. A minor disadvantage of lock slides is the fact that they are an external fixture and thus prevent close stacking of hives or of supers for winter storage.

Straps

Individual lengths of strapping with separate buckles, straps with a fixed single tensioning device and straps with a ratchet tensioner are all commonly used. Straps provide the most expensive solution but are easily removed and do not damage the hive.

▼ EQUIPMENT FOR HARVESTING AND PROCESSING THE HONEY CROP

The equipment described here is used for:

- Clearing the honey storage supers of bees.
- Uncapping, extracting and storing liquid honey.
- Cutting and packing for cut comb.
- Removing and packing sections.
- Re-liquidizing and creaming honey
- Bottling honey

Straps do not damage the hive.

Equipment for clearing the honey storage supers of bees

There are three general methods of removing the honey from the bees:

1 By using chemical repellents to drive the bees out of the supers.
2 By inserting a clearing board with one or more bee escapes.
3 By using smoke as a repellent and brushing the remaining bees off each comb.

Chemical Repellents

Chemical repellents were popular in the past. the usual one used was the carbolic cloth. The carbolic cloth was a cover cloth soaked in carbolic acid. When a carbolic cloth was placed over a super, the bees retreated in a few minutes to the next chamber down and the super without bees could be removed.

Bee-go is a modern equivalent of carbolic acid, and is used to soak a clearing cloth in the same way If you use Bee-go be sure to keep the used cloth in a well sealed container as the odour given off, especially if it gets warm, is most unpleasant to put it mildly.

Mechanical Escapes

All bee escapes are intended to allow the bees to leave the super but prevent their return. There are two methods commonly used for this operation. Both methods rely on a board (the clearing board) which seals the super(s) off from the rest of the hive leaving a restricted exit.

There must be **NO** entry for bees into he super(s) being cleared.
If there is they will empty the super(s) for you very quickly.

The clearing board is normally a cover board with the bee escapes fitted into the "*feed holes*" which are usually shaped to accept the Porter bee escape.

The simplest, and least effective, method relies on leaving an unnatural return path. This method is used in the eight way and the improvised escapes described below.

The most effective method uses a mechanical device which physically prevents the return of the bees. This method is used in the Porter and Round escapes described below.

The Eight Way Escape

The eight way escape is a device which allows the bees to leave the super through eight narrowing, radial channels. The exits from the eight way escape are just large enough to allow the passage of a bee.

The Improvised Escape

The improvised escape (for want of a better name) allows the bees to leave the super through small holes in one or more corners of the clearing board. these holes often have a maze as an entrance and exit.

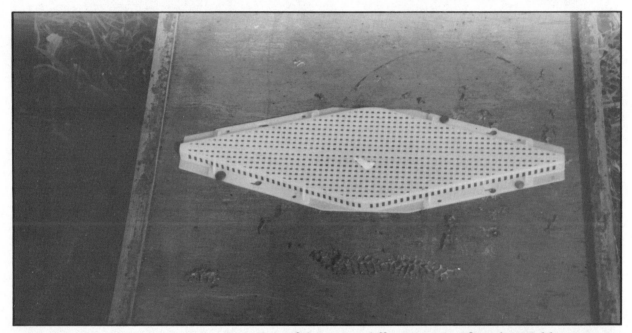

Two of the many different types of mechanical bee escape.

The Porter Escape

The Porter bee escape comprises a small box containing a pair of spring strips through which the bees can push their way in one direction (out of the super). The Porter escape has a top entrance and side exit. It fits in the holes of the cover board converting the cover board into a clearing board which is placed under the super to be cleared of bees.

The Round Escape

The round bee escape comprises a box, larger than the porter escape, which is similar in design and operation to the spray entrance. The round escape has top entry and side exit like the porter escape but these are separated with light angled "*fingers*" which the bees can push their way under. The "*fingers*" fall back into place and prevent the bees returning to the honey storage super. The round escape is fitted into a clearing board and is used in the same way as a porter bee escape.

A special brush with soft hairs (a bee brush) may be used to brush off the few remaining bees when the frames are being removed from the cleared supers.

Uncapping Equipment

When combs intended for extraction have been cleared of bees they must have their wax cappings removed.

For the process of uncapping you need:

1 A tool to remove the cappings
2 A tank or tray which will allow honey to drain out of the removed cappings
3 Somewhere to put the uncapped frames

Tools

There is a wide choice of tools available for uncapping the sealed frames, these include:

Sharp long special purpose knives
Heated knives, electric or hot water
Uncapping forks, straight or cranked
Improvised tools i.e. an electric carving knife with only a single blade fitted

The uncapping forks are most useful for frames with an undulating surface

Uncapping Tank and Strainer

During the process of uncapping some honey is removed with the wax cappings or drips out of the frame. The strainer is used to separate this honey from the wax cappings.

For small and medium scale beekeeping operations, a polythene tank which holds about 70lbs of honey and is fitted with a honey gate (large bore tap) is used for several purposes. One use of this tank, when fitted with a strainer bag, is as a cappings strainer.

The strainer bag overlaps the top of the tank and is held in position by means of a draw string round the outside of the tank. a piece of wood across the top of the tank supports the frame while you are uncapping it. The cappings and some honey drop into the bag and the surplus honey drains through into the tank.

Uncapping Tray

An uncapping tray is an alternative to the tank and strainer described above. A heated tray is used to separate any honey from the wax cappings. The uncapping tray also serves as a drip tray the uncapped frames being supported above the tray until they are put into the extractor.

Uncapping Machines

For larger scale operations a machine with a reciprocating blade is used for uncapping.

Extractors

Most forms of honey extractor rely on the fact that when the bees build the cells to store honey in they do not make them horizontal but angled slightly upwards.

This is one reason to make sure your hives are level.

NOTE: as the normal frame alignment is back to front, a slight tilt forwards to ensure that water does not collect on the floorboard does not affect the cell angle for extracting purposes.

Honey extractors spin the uncapped frames which have been loaded into a central cage and the honey is thrown out by centrifugal force.

There are three types of honey extractor in common use for small scale beekeeping:

1 Tangential
2 Radial
3 Parallel radial

The Tangential Extractor

The uncapped frames to be extracted are mounted in the tangential extractor with one side of the uncapped comb facing outward.

There are two sub types of tangential extractor, one in which the frames are mounted with the top bar uppermost (as in the hive) and one in which the frames are mounted with one side bar uppermost.

The type in which the frames are mounted with one side bar uppermost should be loaded such that the bottom bar leads in the direction of rotation.

Tangential extractors extract only one side of each frame at a time. As the honey in the side of the frame not being extracted exerts a force on the wax mid rib of the comb, it is necessary to frequently reverse the comb and extract from each side alternately to prevent the wax comb from breaking.

For the same reason the rotation needs to be fairly slow when the frames being extracted are full.

Tangential extractors hold two to eight shallow frames and many are capable of extracting from deep frames.

Radial Extractors

The uncapped frames to be extracted are mounted in the radial extractor with the top bar outermost and one side bar uppermost.

This type of extractor relies entirely on the angle of the cells for its operation, the honey "*peeling*" out with the effect of centrifugal force.

Radial extractors extract the honey from both sides of the frames at the same time and therefore eliminate the necessity to reverse the combs

Radial extractors for small scale operations hold eight to twenty frames. The smallest diameter radials hold eight to twelve shallow frames, slightly larger machines hold twenty shallow or ten deep frames.

Smaller radial extractors can be fitted with a cage which enables deep frames to be extracted tangentially.

Parallel Radial Extractors

The uncapped frames to be extracted are mounted in parallel radial extractor with the top bar outermost and one side of the uncapped frame uppermost.

The parallel radial extractor holds two or three shallow frames.
This type of extractor is similar in operation to the radial described above.

The manual polythene radial extractor

Other Types of Extractor

Other types of extractor exist and are used mainly for large scale operations.

A modified spin drier can be used to separate honey from wax when combs have been cut out of their frames. The honey/wax must be at a suitable temperature to prevent wax passing through the lining cloth which has been fitted to the spin drier.

Power Sources and Construction

All of the above types are available with manual or electric drives
and constructed of polythene or stainless steel. The powered versions allow the uncapping of the next load during extraction which reduces the overall time for the extraction process.

Settling Tanks

Settling tanks are sometimes used to remove any air bubbles or wax particles from the honey before it is put into storage containers or jars. In the latter case it is sometimes referred to as a bottling tank. Ideally, the settling tank is tall and has a small diameter with a honey gate type tap just above the base. For small scale operations, the tank previously described for uncapping may be used as a settling tank.

Honey Storage

Honey can be stored for long periods (years) providing that fermentation can be prevented.

Fermentation occurs as a natural reaction between yeast and a sugar solution.
Wild yeasts are accidentally introduced into the hive by the bees, and honey (mainly fructose and glucose) contains water.

If the water content is less than about 18% the honey will not ferment. The bees cap the cells with wax when the honey is concentrated to this level and so honey extracted from capped cells is unlikely to ferment.

One method of preventing fermentation of honey with a higher water content is to heat it to a temperature which will kill the yeast. This method will destroy some of the other contents, the honey will be darkened in colour and will become less viscous. Although this method is sometimes used commercially, it results in a lower quality product and is therefore not recommended.

Containers for Storage

Containers used for the storage of honey must be constructed of material which will not contaminate the contents. The permitted materials are: food grade polythene, stainless steel and glass.
If the stored honey is to be heated at a later date, the containers should be of a type which will be suitable for the temperature to be used and should be of a size that will fit the container that you are going to heat them in.

Processing Honey

Stored honey will granulate as described in Chapter 2. In order to bottle honey which has granulated it must be either reliquified or partially reliqufied and "creamed". The honey will therefore need to be heated.

Honey is a poor conductor of heat and if granulated honey is placed in a high temperature environment, local overheating will occur before the parts most remote from the heat source become liquid.

When you reliquify honey, the only way to maintain the original quality is to heat it at a temperature of about 100 degrees Fahrenheit for a long time. The actual time required will depend on the quantity of honey in the container and to some extent, the shape of the container. The shape of the container has an effect as it will govern the distance the heat has to travel to the solid honey in the centre.

As a general guide to the time needed to reliquify, 1lb glass jars would take about a half to one hour, a 10lb cubic polythene container would take two or three hours.

Remember that the honey will retain its heat and continue to liquify for a long time after it has been removed from the heat source.

If you are partially reliquifing the honey so that you can cream it, it is best to reliquify several containers of honey, one at a time, so that you can vary the state in which you remove them from the heat source. If any are too liquid but still warm you can remove the next with more solid honey in it to get the final mix right.

Equipment for Reliquifing Granulated Honey

At the present time there is no equipment available for reliquifing honey on a small scale. Most beekeepers use an improvised water bath or heated cupboard.

Honey which has granulated in the comb can be reliquified and separated from the wax on a heated uncapping tray.

Honey which has granulated in a storage container can be reliquified in a water bath or in a heated cupboard.

The Water Bath

The simplest version of the water bath is a saucepan partially filled with water and with one or more pieces of wood in the bottom.

If the granulated honey is in a container with an air tight lid, the lid should be loosened to prevent an explosion. The lid should not be removed as water vapour, and possibly water, will get into the honey.

The container should be insulated from the direct heat which will be applied to the saucepan by placing it on the wood.

The water level should be as high as possible to conduct the heat into the maximum amount of honey, but should not be so high that it can get into the container.

The heat applied should be the minimum required to slowly liquify the honey.

This method has the disadvantage that the heat is normally difficult to control. Overheating and the resultant loss of quality can easily occur.

The Heated Cabinet

A heated cabinet can be constructed with a low heat source and with thermostatic temperature control.

The cabinet should be well insulated. An old refrigerator or freezer is suitable for use as a heated cabinet.

The heat source can be a low wattage electric lamp. A hot water tank external thermostat can be used to control the temperature at about 100 ˚F/40 ˚C.

Equipment for Creaming Honey

The tank used for uncapping, settling and bottling can also be used as a container for creaming honey. The honey to be creamed should be mainly liquid (say 90 to 95%) the crystallised remainder being soft enough for you to break up and mix with the liquid.

The amount of mixing should be limited, An electric food mixer will break up the crystals too much and should not be used.

The simplest device for creaming is a wooden spoon.

A special purpose honey creamer is a device like a large potato masher. The honey creamer is very effective for creaming 30 to 60lbs of honey in the general purpose tank.

Equipment for Bottling Honey

For small scale operations the general purpose tank is suitable for bottling honey. The honey gate fitted to this tank is most important when bottling as you will want a fast cut off of the honey. There are a number of variations of the honey gate and it is worth while getting a good one if you intend to use the general purpose tank for bottling.

▼ EQUIPMENT FOR OTHER HIVE PRODUCTS

1 Wax

As previously stated you will get wax as a by-product of any beekeeping operation. It is good apiary hygiene to collect the surplus wax, and having collected it you might as well make good use of it.

In order to use wax it needs to be separated from most of the impurities e.g. pollen propolis and cell "*varnish*", which will be mixed with it. Wax is easily separated from impurities when it is in the liquid state.

There are several devices available for melting the wax and separating it from impurities some of these types are described below:

Solar types comprise a wooden box with a double glazed cover. The wax is placed on an inclined metal tray, when the heat of the sun melts the wax it runs down the tray, through a strainer and into a container. Solar wax extractors are suitable for dealing with small quantities and cost nothing to run.
Steam types comprise a metal tank with a perforated inner tank. The wax is placed in the perforated inner tank, water in the outer tank is boiled and the steam melts the wax. The molten wax passes through the perforations and is channelled to a spout. A container is placed under the spout to collect the wax. Steam type wax extractors are suitable for dealing with larger quantities of wax (several pounds at a time).

You can improvise a wax extractor for small quantities of wax as follows:

Place the wax in a "*bag*" which will strain it when it is molten.

A suitable "*bag*" can be a nylon stocking or "*Tight leg*".

Place a weight in with the wax to stop the bag floating when it is empty.

Place the bag containing wax and weight into a saucepan, (a double saucepan is safest) cover well with water and boil. **DO NOT** allow the mixture to boil over, remember that wax is flammable. When the wax has melted remove the saucepan from the heat source. The wax will float to the surface and solidify. **DO NOT** attempt to reheat as the wax will have sealed the water in the bottom of the saucepan.

2 Pollen

Pollen traps may be fitted to the hive entrance. A pollen trap comprises a wire mesh which brushes the pollen off the legs of the returning worker bees, and a container which the pollen falls into.

The use of pollen traps should be limited and the hives inspected regularly to ensure that sufficient pollen is available for brood rearing.

3 Propolis

Bees will fill any small gaps in the hive with propolis. A screen is available which has gaps of a size that the bees will fill with propolis. This screen may be placed under the cover board and removed when it has been filled.

▼ EQUIPMENT FOR COLONY PROTECTION

This equipment has been covered in the section on colony protection. The main items are:

- Protection from overheating
- Travelling screens and ventilated floors
- Protection from starvation
- Feeders and candy (see Appendix D)
- Protection from enemies
- Mouse guards

▼ MISCELLANEOUS EQUIPMENT

There are many items of miscellaneous equipment to be found in the equipment manufacturers catalogues.

Examples of this category are:

- Queen marking cages and paint.

The queen marking cage in use.

Chapter 8

WHERE TO LEARN MORE

These notes tell you about:

1 Local and national beekeeping associations, what they do and where to find them.
2 Specialist beekeeping libraries.
3 Books both for beginners and on specialist subjects
4 Other sources of information

Associations can be divided into Local and National associations.

▼ LOCAL ASSOCIATIONS

The local associations provide a forum for discussion with other local beekeepers. The local associations normally organise practical demonstrations at monthly intervals during the summer, and organise lectures on beekeeping topics at monthly intervals in the winter.

By joining a local association before you get your bees you can go to the practical demonstrations. This is one of the best ways of learning how to perform some of the basic manipulations.

There are usually other advantages of local association membership which vary from asociation to association.

Some examples of these advantages are:

- Training courses for beginners.
- Training courses in advanced beekeeping.
- Disease examinition equipment and/or facilities.
- Equipment purchase discounts.
- Equipment available for loan/hire (e.g. honey extractors).
- Insurance via national association (see national association).
- Migratory beekeeping sites.
- Local, competitive, produce shows.

▼ NATIONAL ASSOCIATIONS

The national association provides higher level facilities for example:

- Representation to government, the EEC and international bodies.
- Communication via local association represetives and magazine.
- Insurance, third party, loss of stock, and product liability.
- Education, by setting standards and organising examinations.
- Marketing, by conducting market surveys.
- Publicity for beekeeping.
- National library services.
- National, competitive, produce shows.

▼ OTHER USEFUL ORGANISATIONS

International Bee Research Association (IBRA)

(CONBA)

▼ SPECIALIST BEEKEEPING LIBRARIES

The MOIR library Edinburgh
Controlled by the Scottish Beekeepers Association.
Location: George IV Bridge under the Music Library.

The IBRA (International Bee Research Association) library
Controlled by the IBRA

▼ GENERAL AND SPECIFIC TOPIC BOOKS

There are many thousands of books on beekeeping and related subjects. A few of the most useful and some of the standard reference works are listed below, those most suitable for beginners are listed under General:

SUBJECT	AUTHOR	TITLE
General	Hooper	A Guide to bees and Honey
General	Couston	Principles of practical beekeeping
General	SBA	An Introduction to Bees and Beekeeping
Honey	Crane E	Honey
Pollen	Hodges D	The Pollen Loads of the Honeybee
Wax	Cogshall & Morse	Beeswax
Wax	Brown	Beeswax
Queen Rearing	Snelgrove	Queen Rearing
Physiology & Anatomy	Snodgrass	Anatomy and Physiology of The Honeybee
Anatomy	Dade	Anatomy and Dissection of the Honeybee
History	Crane	The Archaeology of Beekeeping
History	Fraser	Beekeeping in Antiquity
Senses	Butler	The Honeybee an Introduction to her Senses, Physiology and Behaviour

APPENDIX A

MOVING BEES

The factors relevant to moving bees are :

1 The homing instinct of bees.
2 The amount of heat generated by a confined colony.
3 Securing the hive for transport

The Homing Instinct of Bees

Bees can fly over an area within about a 3 mile radius of their hive and return to within a few inches of the entrance.   If there are no other distracting hives close to the hive to be moved, they will eventually locate their own hive if it is moved by only 3 or 4 feet.

If the bees have been confined to their hive for several days, for example by bad weather, they will re-orient themselves when they leave the hive again.

If they find a temporary obstruction at the entrance which they must clear, they will usually re-orient themselves. The hive entrance is sometimes deliberatly blocked with grass to achieve this effect.

The Amount of Heat Generated by a Confined Colony

Bees generate a great deal of heat. Excess heat is normally removed by the circulation of air through the hive. Air circulation is achieved by fanning bees drawing cool air in at one side and expelling hot air at the other side.

The amount of heat produced by a confined colony can easily raise the temperature to a level which is sufficient to melt the wax comb.

The confined colony must therefore be allowed access to sufficient air to cool the inside of the hive.

The amount of ventilation required depends on the ambient temperature, the length of time that the bees are to be confined and the strength of the colony.

The maximum ventilation is provided by the use of a travelling screen and a ventilated floorboard.

Securing The Hive For Transport

There are many methods of securing hives for transport, a few of the more popular are given here.

First of all the two cheapest.

The use of thin strips of wood up the outside of the hive bend nailed to each moveable part of the hive: the floor, each chamber of the hive and the cover board or traveling screen.
The use of staples between each moveable part.

Lock Slides.

Shaped metal brackets are accurately screwed to the sides of the hive parts and a shaped metal wedge is driven between them. The metal wedge pulls the hive parts together. Lock slides have declined in popularity with the advent of special straps.

Straps.

There are at least 3 types of strap which completly go round the hive and are capable of being tightened.

The original straps had a separate buckle through which the strap was threaded and tensioned. Subsequent types have a tensioning lever or a ratchet.

Guidelines for Moving Bees

Make sure the joints in the hive are "*bee tight*".

Secure the hive parts so that they will stay "*bee tight*".

Close the hive entrance in the evening when flying has finished or in the early morning before flying starts (evening is safer).

A cover board ventilated with some perforated material such as zinc or plastic over the two feed holes, provides sufficient ventilation if transport is in cool weather and is late at night or in the early morning. **IF IN DOUBT USE A TRAVELLING SCREEN.**

A floor with some holes covered with similar perforated material can be used for additional ventilation.

Close the entrance securely. Polyurethene (seat cushion) foam is sometimes used, a ventilated board nailed to the front is better, a heather floor with a closing device is even better.

Try to provide a cooling air flow past the hives if possible.

You can stand the hive in the inverted roof for transport.

APPENDIX B

NOTES ON ASSEMBLY OF HIVE PARTS

The Floor - Smith or National

The finished floor is reversible to provide a deep or shallow entrance. For this reason the floorboard groves in the side rails are off-center. You need to make sure that you fix them both the same way up.

The floor boards should go from the back to the front of the side rails, any shortage can be adjusted with the stepped section.

National floorboards often have more than one stepped section.

Two pins stop the entrance block from pushed back into the hive.

The thick back rail goes on the wide entrance side.

The thin back rail goes on the narrow entrance side.

Brood Chambers/Shallow Honey Storage Supers

Smith

The inside corners are often numbered (1 goes to 1, 2 to 2 etc).

Before nailing check:

Handles are the right way up and on the outside.

Ledges for frame supports are opposite each other.

Box is square (diagonals are equal). It is advisable to check this several times during nailing.

National

Make sure that the two plain sides (shorter pieces of wood) which fit into the slots in the other two sides. are fixed 11/16 inch (17mm) below the tops of the slotted sides. This is to guarantee the correct spacing between the tops of the frames in one box and the bottom of the frames in the box above.

The outer end rail with both top and bottom flat is the upper one. This is used as a "*handle*" when lifting.

The sloping part of the other (lower) end rail is the top of that rail. This is to allow rain to run off more easily.

Check that the box is square (diagonals are equal) before and during nailing.

Roof - Smith or National

Insulation goes between plywood and metal cover.

Vent slots go at the top with the slope down to the outside. This is to allow rain to run off more easily.

Make sure that the vent gauze is fitted securely so that it is beeproof. If it is not robbing could occur under some conditions.

APPENDIX C

MAKING UP A FRAME

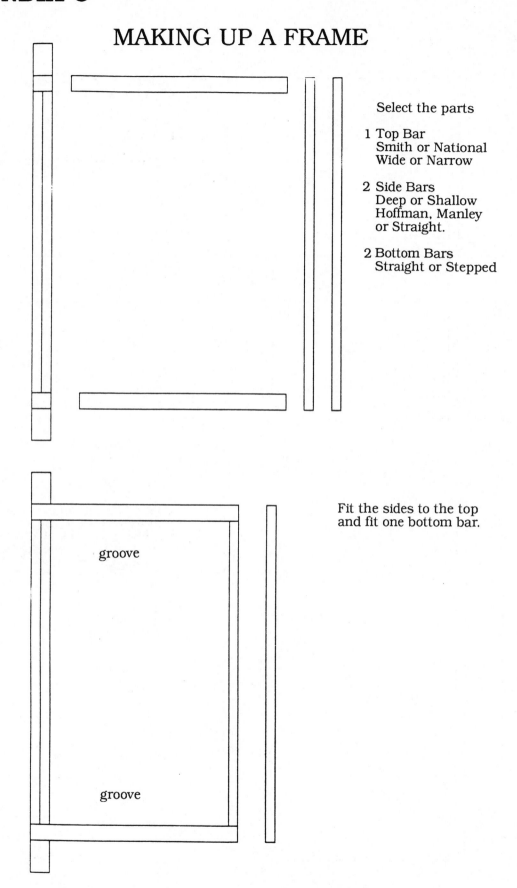

Select the parts

1 Top Bar
Smith or National
Wide or Narrow

2 Side Bars
Deep or Shallow
Hoffman, Manley
or Straight.

2 Bottom Bars
Straight or Stepped

groove

groove

Fit the sides to the top
and fit one bottom bar.

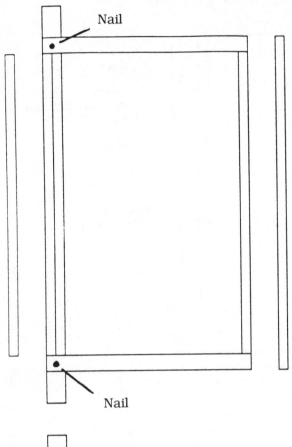

Nail

Nail

Remove the wedge piece from the top bar.

Make sure the frame is square.

Nail the sides to the top.

Fit a sheet of foundation into the slots in the side bar and into the step in the top bar (where the wedge will grip it).

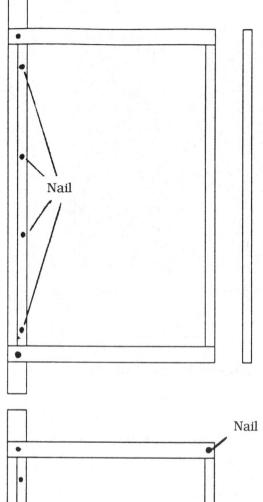

Replace the wedge and
nail it firmly into place.

Nail

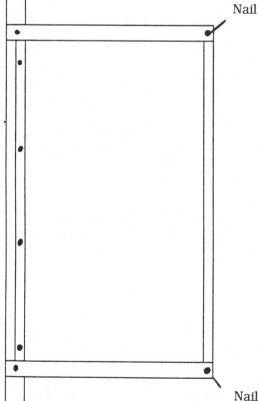

Nail

Fit the second bottom bar,
check that the frame is
still square and nail the
bottom bars firmly.

NOTE: The correct way to
nail the bottom bars for
maximum strength is as
shown in the figure, i.e.
through both bottom bars.
With this method of
nailing it is very difficult
to remove them if you want
to renew the foundation in
an old frame.
It is common practice to
nail up through each bottom
bar into the side bar.

Nail the bottom bars only
art the ends. The foundation
can stretch and will buckle if
it is not free to move between
the bottom bars.

Nail

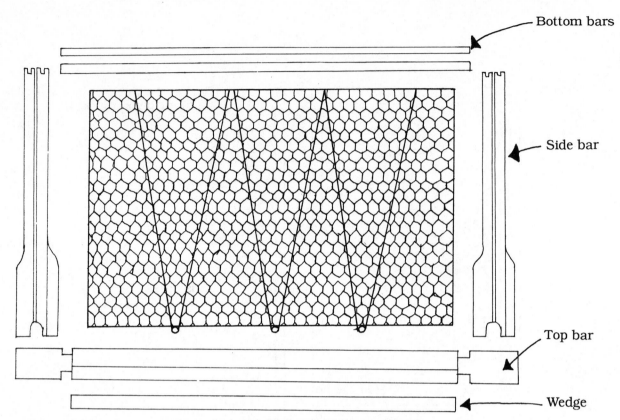

Parts of a British Standard self-spacing brood frame.

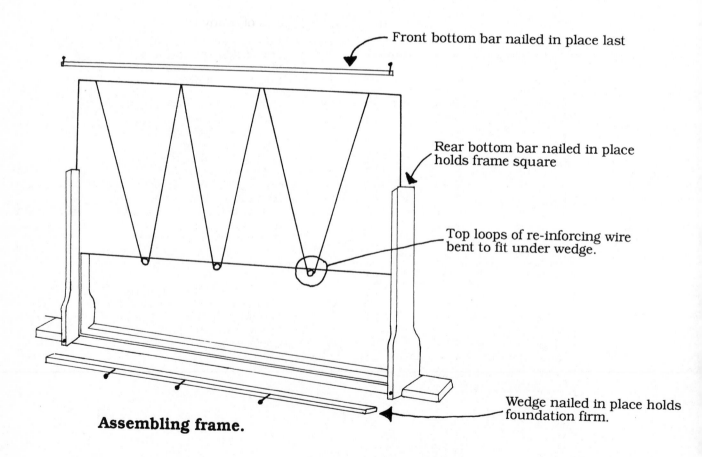

Assembling frame.

74

APPENDIX D

CANDY RECIPE

Ingredients

Granulated Sugar	3lb
Water	1/2 pt
Salt	pinch (optional)
Cream of Tartar	pinch (optional)

Why the optional ingredients ?

Bees have a preference for slightly salted water.

Sugar is inverted by boiling with cream of tartar, this saves the bees inverting it themselves.

Making The Candy

Put the sugar in a pan. Add the boiling water and stir, the mixture will be thick. Continue to stir while heating until the mixture becomes thin. **DO NOT** allow the sugar to burn (or caramelise) as this will produce a toxic candy.

Add the salt and cream of tartar and allow to simmer for 20 minutes.

Grease the dishes you are going to to cast the blocks of candy in.

Stir the mixture as it is cooling and when it begins to thicken, pour it into the greased dishes.

NOTE that it will thicken more quickly as you are pouring it as there is less candy to hold the heat.

Allow to set.

The finished blocks of candy should be soft enough for you to be able to mark them with your finger nail, but firm enough to tip out and handle.

APPENDIX E

WHAT YOU NEED TO REMEMBER

THE MOST IMPORTANT

Your first responsibility is the welfare of your livestock

COLONY PROTECTION

Protection from:

Enemies	Use mouse guards in winter. Use entrance blocks for wasps/robbing bees in late summer.
Loss of Queen	Remove queen excluder for winter
Crop Spraying	Use a spray entrance to confine to the hive. Make sure there is a source of water available.
Internally generated heat	Spray entrance/ventilated floor and when confined to the hive traveling screen depending on the ambient temperature.
Starvation	Regular checks, feeding if necessary particularly in the spring.
Disease	Do not feed honey from an unknown source. Have a health check on stray swarms.
Dampness	Use good waterproof hives.

THE SECOND MOST IMPORTANT

To prevent nuisance and ensure a surplus crop

SWARM PREVENTION OR CONTROL

Prevention   Before swarm preparations have been started.

Use Demaree method or one of its developments.
AND PREVENT SWARMING
OR Divide the colony **AND HOPE**
OR Give adequate storage space **AND PRAY.**

Control	Inspect at regular intervals and take action when swarm prepara tions have started.
	Make artificial swarm.
	You chose to make increase or unite later. You can extend the period between inspections by clipping the queens wings to delay swarming until one of the new queens emerge.

You determine the number of colonies (queens) by using the relationship between:

> Swarm control,
> Queen rearing,
> Making an increase and
> Uniting.

OTHER IMPORTANT POINTS

Quality of construction	Nail frames securely. Make up the hive parts accurately. Leave a bee space.
Be safe and confident	Get good protective clothing.
Learn more	Join the local association. Go to practical demonstrations. Meet and learn from other beekeepers. Join the national association. Use the national (Moir) library. Read the Scottish Beekeeper.

Get your bees in the spring. A nucleus is an easy way to start with fewer bees and virtually no risk of swarming in the first season.

If you have a full colony, get enough equipment to make an artificial swarm, or to hive a natural swarm. (A spare floor, deep, 11 frames with foundation, coverboard and roof)

If you have two colonies, you can recover if one is found to be a drone layer in the spring.

MAKING AN INCREASE

The easiest way to make an increase is to deliberatly create the conditions for swarming and then practice swarm control.

To create the conditions for swarming restrict the colony to a single brood chamber. You can speed up the process by feeding.

Check every week for queen cells and when they occur make an artificial swarm.